This book belongs to

.... Skyler ....

There are hidden acorns throughout the pages of this book.
May seeking the acorn serve as a reminder of the joy found in
reading good books and finding hidden treasures.

Heart to Heart **Publishing, Inc.**

Heart to Heart Publishing, Inc.
528 Mud Creek Road • Morgantown, KY 42261
(270) 526-5589
www.hearttoheartpublishinginc.com

Author: Debra Luke Hardison
Artist: Donna Brooks
Senior Editor: L .J. Gill
Editor: Susan J. Mitchell
Copy-Editor: Nicki Bishop
Layout: April Yingling-Jernigan

First Edition
10 9 8 7 6 5 4 3 2

Heart to Heart Publishing, Inc. books are available at a special discount for
bulk purchases in the US by corporations, institutions and other organizations.
For more information, please contact Special Sales at 270-526-5589.

Printed 2017. Batch number: 79217-0. Printed by Shenzhen Caimei Printing Co., Ltd., Nanling, China

Dedication:

For my children, Jarrod and Jordan.
May you always remain curious.
Thank you for making a difference.

- Debra Luke Hardison

Old friends are jewels in our lives.
Deb is one friend that is very special to me.
Hope this sweet story reaches many, many children.

- Donna Brooks

DROPSY

Written By

Debra Luke Hardison

Illustrated By

Donna Brooks

One beautiful fall day,
outside was a girl.
When down from a tree
fell a small baby squirrel.

Surprised, she looked up to the tree behind them. Was his momma up there trying to find him?

There was no one there,
but Jordan knew what to do,
a squirrel needs to be fed
and kept warm, too.

First, she asked mommy
if it was ok to keep him,
for without food and shelter
his body would weaken.

13

Mommy said yes,
but since he was a squirrel,
later he would need
to return to his world.

We knew it was best
for squirrels to be free.
Jordan named him Dropsy,
since he fell from a tree.

Book of
Squirrels

17

Jordan's friend Olivia
helped out as he grew.
He was fun to play with,
but could be annoying, too!

Jarrod made many trips
to buy Dropsy more milk.
He loved to hold him -
his fur felt like silk.

The weather turned cold
and snow fell down.
Dropsy stayed inside,
not out on the ground.

23

He curled up in his cage
at bedtime each night.

25

Spent some days in Mommy's pocket, much to his delight!

Spring finally came and
brought with it flowers.
He would sit by the window
and stare out for hours.

We took Dropsy outside,
he could run really fast.
He played out in the yard
with nature at last!

Each day he played outside
longer and longer.
He learned to climb trees and
grew stronger and stronger.

Then one day Dropsy
climbed to the top of a tree
And turned to say goodbye -
Finally he was free.

34

SQUIRREL FACTS

Before they are born/after their birth...
- Squirrels build nests of twigs and leaves.
- Nests can be up to a foot wide.
- Female squirrels give birth one or two times per year.
- Eastern gray squirrels may be born in late winter/early sp...
- A newborn squirrel is about an inch long.
- Baby squirrels are called kittens.
- Kittens are born toothless, blind and naked.
- They begin eating regular food around six to 10 weeks old.

The life of a squirrel...
- If a squirrel lives past the first year of life, they usually live 5-10 years.
- Squirrels are small to medium sized rodents.
- There are 285 species of squirrels.
- Flying squirrels don't really fly – they glide through the air when they jump from tree to tree.
- Flying squirrels have been known to glide for as many as 295 feet (they can also make 180 degree turns while gliding).

Where they live/What they eat...
- They may live in trees, but they are capable of living in every habitat on earth.
- Squirrels eat a range of nuts, seeds, and fruits, along with insects, eggs, snakes and birds, depending on the species.
- They famously store food for winter in secret spots around their homes.
- Squirrels can survive most anywhere, even in modern cities.

- Facts.net/squirrel

ACORN ANSWERS

Page 6: In cloud. Page 7: In leaf, top left. Page 8: Lower left corner. Page 9: On branch by squirrel. Page 10: On lower left side. Page 11: On squirrel's tummy. Page 12: Under upper leaf. Page 13: In girl's hand. Page 14: In cloud, upper left cloud under leaf. Page 15: On cuff of Mom's shirt. Page 16: Bottom left corner. Page 17: Over Mom's left shoulder on chair Page 18: Middle lower page. Page 19: Between girl's arm. Page 20: Upper left page. Page 21: On milk can. Page 22: On upper window seal. Page 23: In girl's hair; In top window page. Page 24: Upper right corner. Page 25: On front side of cage. Page 26: On button. Page 27: On pocket. Page 28: Lower middle of page. Page 29: Inside cup. Page 30: Bottom left corner. Page 31: On squirrel's rump. Page 32: On leaf. Page 33: In squirrel's hand. Page 34: On branch. Page 35: Above squirrel's head.

Debra Luke Hardison is the mother of two adult children Jarrod and Jordan. She is a registered nurse, author and life coach who is passionate about nature and the protection of all life. She has been a caretaker to many animals over the years and has come to believe that nature is spiritual and can provide a refuge that allows the imagination to run wild.

Visit the author at www.dropsythesquirrel.com
Twitter: www.twitter.com/@DebraHardison
Facebook: www.facebook.com/debra.l.hardison
Instagram: www.instagram.com/imdebra
LinkedIn: www.linkedin.com/in/debra-luke-hardison-59948263

Donna Brooks was born in Dodge City, Kansas. After twelve years she moved to Kentucky and resides there still. She is blessed with her husband (Billy Joe), two son's (Bryan and Brad), and two grandchildren (Abby and Ethan). Having studied art at Minneapolis Art Institute, she also enriched her studies through work with artists Fred Eliers, W.A. Ballou, Daniel Smith, and Edward Aldrich.

Donna's work has been published in a variety of forms:
• Illustrated children's books
• Cross-stitch patterns for Lean'n Tree note cards
• Porcelain products with Ardleigh Elliot
• Fine art prints with Home Interiors and Home & Garden Party
• She was nominated for the New Artist of the Year Award for collector plates with Bradford Exchange.

Her love of God, people, nature, and animals continues to inspire her painting and work.
www.donnaheathbrooks.com